The Golem Verses

poems by **Diane R. Wiener**

NINE MILE PRESS

Publisher: Nine Mile Art Corp at http://www.ninemile.org
Editors: Bob Herz, Stephen Kuusisto, Andrea Scarpino
Cover Art by Lucy Loo Wales, "Beanstalk Swing with Molecules."
Artist's website is: http://www.lucyloowales.com/

The publishers gratefully acknowledge support of the New York State
Council on the Arts with the support of Governor Andrew M. Cuomo
and the New York State Legislature. We also acknowledge support of
the County of Onondaga and CNY Arts through the Tier Three Project
Support Grant Program. We have also received significant support
from the Central New York Community Foundation. This publication
would not have been possible without the generous support of these
groups. We are very grateful to them all.

ISBN-10: 0-9976147-9-X
ISBN-13: 978-0-9976147-9-4
First edition

Some of these poems were previously published in *Nine Mile Magazine*
and in *Wordgathering: A Journal of Disability Poetry and Literature*.

Special thanks to Elizabeth Anne Socolow and Clark A. Pomerleau.

NEW YORK
STATE OF
OPPORTUNITY.

Council on
the Arts

For my mother,

for my friends and family,

and in loving memory of Aunt Joan.

Contents

A Note to the Reader

In some facets of Jewish culture, Golems are among the fantastical figures that influence our sense of reality. They are, in a way, lifeless and immortal, dead but not zombies. In order for them to become animated, spiritual power words might be written across their (sometimes muddy, possibly wooden) foreheads; at other times, mystical invocations are placed within their mouths.

As releasers of cosmic time, space, and imagination, they can visit you, make things go bump in the night, or disappear from your drawers and then reappear in your closets. Golems can take you anywhere, make you think nearly anything. They might even have the power to put you in touch with the sensation of being inside a black hole, although they were invented (or, if you prefer, noticed) before we knew about black holes.

Golems have been among us since the Middle Ages.

In these poems, I welcome a Golem as a friend, traveling with her wherever she takes me, terrifying, unfamiliar, and, yes, as familiar as vegetables.

While Golems have at times been depicted as limited in speech or as voiceless, and even as unintelligent, the Golem in these poems is quite actively an addresser, an addressee, and a subject. If she is disabled, which is debatable, her disablement is an accepted, integrated part of her wild identities and honest labors.

Diane R. Wiener, 2018

1. The Golem Verses

Verse 1

Watching octopus kites

a new interiority forms

listening to bricolage poems

remembering murdering a tiny golem with my lover

in lucid dreams.

How it bled, made of something other than mud

its flesh responsive to the scalpel.

Even a golem can't protect this vagabond shtetl heart.

Why not just erase the name from its forehead to release it?

Why punish its unintended helplessness?

Invasions cannot always be prevented.

I surrender.

Verse 2

Belligerent ethics prevent me from eating a Golem
killed in dreams.

Before raging collaboration, afraid to cook,
too anxious to consume.

Wrote about Dybbuk, Golem, my variously undead heritage.

Although I no longer eat chicken soup,
I can still produce schmaltz.

Excess becomes familiar, even delicious.

Hyperbole, more functional than merely stereotypical,
is obvious, absurd.

Not just grease.

I tell the Golem, old habits die hard.

Verse 3

Learning how to fish
Golem sings to the seas
High up in trees over the Palisades,
three landscapes concurrent.
Perches for rescued birds,
mounted on the walls of a dark green room,
ramps and tunnels leading to narrow steps
tubing upward and barely passable,
negotiating time, flattening.
Always nearly a new home.

Verse 4

Posing as topiary
Golem fashions herself as several gargoyles
three Yetis
innumerable foliate Bodhisattvas
believing she can be anything
moving while sessile
temporarily sandy
water in hardy supply

Verse 5

Golem joins me, we ask questions.

What spatial, tactile, and linguistic messages could be used to assure that everyone has access to the news about colliding neutron stars, without sight or sound?

Astrophysicists explain the vibrations, and, yes, I am relieved, as I was with learning of solar eclipses' multisensory lives.

There's even an app.

A lattice, my hands, depicts shadowed crescents on cement, the fascism and eugenics so prevalent in the news are again refused.

I remain conflicted about astronomy, considering people without food or shelter.

The discovery of the origins of the universe nevertheless is unmistakably profound.

If gold and platinum shatter in fragments careening off colliding neutron stars, those bits swallowed up by the black holes left behind are likely inhabited by fairies.

Devonian remains of molluscs might have lithic gold and platinum traces, for all we know.

But the poetics of the first question seem lost, Golem thinks, quietly beside me in the woods.

We are, after all, talking about the music of the stars.

Verse 6

Golem and I become one subject, comrades twinned.
Solace in pale hues, a new weird land, familiar.
Finally, I know what tired feels like,
not just how it means.
No sled to drive me home, flying.
No bottled messages, thrown, oceanic.
Sit still and deal the damned Aces.
I don't think so.
No way to the lion wardrobe
no owls
no garden secrets
no safe magic
for tonight.

Verse 7

Odd, imagination labors,
you break the wind eyes,
I smooth the flat sheets of here again are we,
it's always been this way,
as if we didn't just create each other.
Regressus corners beveled,
egrets find all of this funny, defined.
Inside remains the message,
replete defiant lies claim that we never were and cannot be, Golem,
a grammar refused or declared.
We make it up, alone,
pervasive love reappearing in metallic blue anchors,
our private wordless Zohar.

Verse 8

Odd imagination labors, changes,
slight, emphatic.
Surreal ressuscité.
You break the wind eyes; I smooth the flat sheets of
here again are we.
It's always been this way,
as if we didn't just create each other,
never were and cannot be, Golem, our own grammar.
We make it all up,
then metallic love reappears,
anchors a Zohar.

Verse 9

Golem becomes a flour sifter,
so I can pass through the needle eyed sieve,
wet removed,
dry shiny leavings,
headache surprises,
so many lonely creations from a cranial middle ground,
isolated dusty isomers,
older than the other sun.
Sometimes, I still smell
the sick yet hardy maple leaves,
smoky traces of a long gone vicious narrative,
too light to stick to this roof,
moss scraped,
rescued.

Verse 10

Once I flew over a giant form on its back and saw it from way up high winking as we soared past its cheekbones hundreds of miles wide diffused into blue nothing but maybe it was you Golem not St. Michael tapping already nearby all along after my brother by energy died and I didn't know yet about left twisting snail survival without intervention or emissaries or sliding over glass without getting cut.

Verse 11

Alarming, thrilling, a relief,
how easily the abstractions fall from your mouth, Golem,
voweled with everything contained, released.
We dogs follow ourselves all of these lives, hoping, and then,
boom,
we are encircled at the tapestry corner,
muddy mouthed, sated.
You laugh when I say I didn't know you were
the Marshmallow Man, hunting ghosts,
despite resemblance to the Tire Guy,
believing your own materials.
No animals or trees were harmed in the making of
this broken record movie.
Tired of being the joker, I set the needle right,
come back into the room to find you
covered in lotus emerging sleep.
I turn out my feet to smile.

Verse 12

My first cane included a protein shake,
knowing some day I may limp nonstop, with needed nutrients.
So obvious that being in the company of poets is impetus
to write,
which is partly where you come from, Golem.
Nobody saves anybody, but finding a seemingly steady place
to store the changing envelopes is a good plan.
Storage here needs no illusion of creased permanence.
You're no phony.
Me neither.

Verse 13

It's possibly time to tell the story, Golem, about the waiting
namesake embryos in the hall of souls, when you as a child
heard them on the carpeted landing where the dog rested,
in between the staircases, called them the same-time children,
your friends, years before liminal or hyle meant anything.

I have been meeting them all my life, recognized.

The letter dyads created world receded as you grew,
returned so much later in the rooms where,
feeling anxious trails of your image in the future present
waiting for you, you stopped eating carrots for awhile
in sympathy,
because slicing life made you cry and disappear
a little too much.

You grew tired of being afraid of yourself.

Nothing should be wrenched from its roots,
but it happens every minute.

You chose and turned over small clouds
becoming stones in your mouth.

You left them for me to find,
taste taught faith.

Verse 14

Of course, our talk brings up
letters, mouths, mud, dogs, survival shapes

without romance.

Rewriting crowned dalets, smearing ink,
remembering unconscious concentration habits,
in-cheek chewing and tongue angling,
I hope I've expressed enough gratitude.

Golem, your name is no mere repetition.

Verse 15

Let's go for a ride.

I'll speak the truth to you, nothing else, in broken strings, wilted beet greens, and the smell of garlic rushing through the house with its own children.

We'll take your sloping roller coaster, though it and I cannot soothe divergent insomnias, or stop that loud banging noise, achy wheel rims, a rusty timing belt mind with its fish eyes, never resting.

I'll watch the marinara sunset, one of your unmitigated joys, before grief became ancillary and was still the ground.

Golem, you say all this to me, but not just because you can, and I let you.

You sense the beanstalk that I nearly climbed away from here, but we both know it's not tall enough to get that far.

We know I'll stay.

Verse 16

I'm afraid, now that I've found you, again, you'll leave.
Maybe I should have thought you to myself.
I don't believe in keeping, Golem,
I collect books that I have no time to read.
Imagining you within this world that can be no one else's,
why tell anyone,
but I want to share
what cannot be held.

Verse 17

Believing I was gone,

remembering my own life,

lightning flashed back, and

I thought the day I was in the middle of having

was a dialed in jukebox

of the day that already had been.

I was in the next life,

an adjacent shelf,

a filmy overlay,

both plain and majestic.

My body was maybe warning me

of terrors to come,

foreshadowing backwards,

an upside down mind

craving special nothing.

Golem, the lightning was you.

Verse 18

Neck cracks,

highway bends, dark,

whatever I do, you rage.

This weather, never up to me,

at once, between poets reading,

elegant silence,

spatial reprieve,

microphone pendants,

crisp intruding light.

Golem welcomes missing marionettes

suspended from vaulted ceilings,

freedom saunters, unremarkable.

We grab a snack.

The strings lose reception, forget the room,
not storing books given, painted schoolgirl chairs,
piles of cardboard yogurt lid inserts turned
into matching games in rain, stacked baseball cards,
stashed comics, pristine Matchbox cars under a plastic plane.

All lined up, the snaps, clips, pulls still work,

nothing neat about them.

Verse 19

Golem, let's have
papery papayas
timely tangerines
glorious guavas
resplendent radishes
aspiring asparagus
nocturnal nectarines
persuasive pomegranates
vibrant vine-ripened tomatoes
courteous cauliflower
beneficent broccoli
profound plums
ornate oranges
gracious, graceful grapes
gladdened grapefruit
splendid starfruit
beauteous bananas
tremendous turnips
political parsnips
amicable apples
engaged, endearing endive
robust romaine
festive figs
appreciative apricots
amiable artichokes.

Verse 20

Metal scraping, vaguely pointy, the spring within
the squeezed flour sifter handles pleases me.
I feel very responsible, doing good work.
I pick up and push down on my shiny shoe right foot,
strengthening my grip.
I have no idea what we baked.
Haven't written about the height I have yet to become.
It's well before I can reach the coveted cardboard box of
flexible straws, the Special K, a yellow napkin holder
stuffed to the gills.
Haven't inherited the painted plates on which we now place,
as usual, perfectly toasted cheese sandwiches
that you cut into quarters for me,
next to our matching cups of tepid Sanka,
and vertically halved paper napkins.
Alone with you, your home the only place
where I'll eat without heartache,
I don't know that, decades later,
Golem brings me back to your kitchen,
at Midnight.

Verse 21

Soul dance teal flattens me,

hours past signs

from the God of my childhood,

in whom I no longer believe,

except when they show up,

sometimes magisterial, often in jeans,

with those faces of gratitude, calling home,

moments after I mention them,

despite irreconcilable differences,

happening later in the night,

attempting to wreck the otherwise sweet train of a day.

Half awake, Golem asks me why peonies wilt

while nightmares spread pollen

once finished with vulture work.

Light jitters even when it's undercover.

Truth isn't slipped through a detector,

but noble daily tries, by tea,

on a split table.

Verse 22

Sometimes, Golem rises,

music swimming in her mind,

knows dreams spread on bread

left some indentations on the cushion,

the now absent music beside them, floats.

Sometimes, riding on the bus,

Golem listens to change clanking in the gumball machine,

where you pay, Yiddish is spoken,

always with eye contact, regardless of sight.

Two kinds of double cataracts separate these landforms from green violinists,

crescents airborne over that ever-present roof.

We travel to the top,

take our seats, swing, look down,

no longer count the stories.

Verse 23

Maybe the monster isn't blue, but it's not news that, once you befriend her, you'll have immediate company, lateral moves when playing rubber band chess with your own internal clanging, learn blankets to warm found habits, fashion fireless reserves, and then, the skinny lion you felted together out of the storybook joins you on trips back to get yourself out of the house, the Golem with you, not yours, there is no monster, aspects unexplained. The other worlds quit billiards, heavens descend unceremoniously, and you accept the breeze, because it's all the same place.

Verse 24

What to write,

which bug eye facet to share,

how to change the light bulb,

after a liberation psalm that isn't a secret,

when five already dead animals of different sizes

get run over, again, on the highway,

because, as we've said, some things can't be prevented,

why the Golem wipes my nearly always unrelaxed brow,

takes my jaw in her hands,

knows less sleep calls forth more reassurance.

Verse 25

You have given me, Golem
more than safe haven
clean forks
return trips
tight buttons.

We think together about things besides
unfurled caterpillars
sick plants
rescued worms
approaching sand.

These are not just lists
affirming strategic refusal
verbs being nouns
double meanings
plaid stamps
fear plays
or even arteries.

I'm done
with hiding places,
preferring refuge.

You move my chin under the word spigot,
the widening faucet washer won't be replaced.

I don't have to be told twice to drink up.

Verse 26

Although we've been advised the clouds are full,

Golem and I take to the sky.

I don't know how it happens,

expecting carpets, escalators, pterodactyls.

The dragons are busy with their seasons, and pay us no mind.

We pass by no echoes,

but know Ironwoods or Mesquites

must have nursed these gigantic Saguaros,

now grown and peppered up top with Opuntia.

There are no dust specks or poppy fields,

Peter Pan has clearly left town.

An egret family watches.

I'm so pleased.

We arrive, sit.

My relief at having nothing to do

reflects a pile of thick old wishes

headed in a dire direction.

I choose another me,

leave familiarity on wet stones

by the edge.

A fleeting allowance,

I accept this cold lake gift,

bite into an apple, rest.

Verse 27

Sounding their own oceans,

streets unforgiving and well meaning

make flotsam of old buses,

strained umbrellas,

dented bins, tossed to wind.

We can't cross the parkway, this time, Golem.

You're busy, mending cracked rooftops,

guarding the last of the nearby hydrangea.

Later, we share bagels, rainbow cookies,

clutching sleep.

Even the cleanest curtains

cannot shadow agitated corners, for long.

Sometimes, giving up is the best grief present.

Verse 28

Nearly didn't make it,

the latest deadline artifice,

more negative assertions,

ways to say fear happens

regardless of knowing

one will likely be alone at their deathbed,

even with a Golem,

welcoming wide egg noodles eaten way too late

with hard cider sipped way too fast.

The words that comfort me tonight are

still, truly, released.

Verse 29

Golem, lately the Saturn impersonator,

but no impostor,

returns on her flying hourglass,

shakes her head at gender,

yells in seven written languages

typed with a stylus,

and throws up caution

without the wind

right after keeping down the good men.

Tired feet must shift apace

on the highest bleachers,

dendrons stretched

beyond this baseball field.

I can't catch on,

sure can't catch,

but, if you ask me to pitch,

no one will be disappointed

on this moonless night.

Verse 30

Now and again, meat is on my mind.
Returning to cabbage skin,
trepidation coated confidence
can't inverse in time to stop the cuts
messing up our fake plans.
Fearful slicing is tiresome,
plunging into the colandered air
a far better bet.
Sea to sea,
Golem does a Dead Man's Float,
I can hardly swim.
What became of the shameful tadpole patch,
the gluey popsicle sticks,
the dry beans bursting out
of the barely assembled trivet?
Presumably in the middle of life,
I'm part saprophyte,
so bring me your rotten yummy wood
yearning to creep free.
We'll liberate the bugs
before the fecund feast.
There will be no cliché grinning
at the setting of the table or the sun.

Verse 31

Left in your not right mind

is the notion that telling

your kind of stories

right before bed

is somehow a good idea.

Even you must know

night breaks up terror

into particulate matter,

reconfigures shadowy shapes,

a set of unexpected knives

thrown about the floor

of a barren house

you don't actually have.

I visited the horror movie garage,

the tree grown through the western wall,

roots upending any hope of foundation.

Golem came by with a whistle,

we fled, easily.

If only I could forget the creatures

blown onto adjacent shores,

swollen gills open,

odd beauty,

sinewed optics intact.

Verse 32

Without barometers or bibles,

remade words percolate,

ground up, pressed,

newsprint putty remainders,

thread in uneven dark wood,

divergent coordinates imperceptible.

Even if I lower the thermostat,

white heat is on,

however many ways there are

to imagine escape, Golem,

we could not care,

get or be lost.

Verse 33

Soaked letters float up from the bottom,

we fold into frogs, flowers,

aiming for crane flaps,

persistent in fierce peace.

Pitches cool flat, turn to sharp soup,

Golem chews her fingertips,

scenes key in.

Chasing red panthers

who before were licking at our heels,

grooming by osmosis more than example,

it's our turn,

pawpads on fire.

Tents collapse,

beasts and water bearers led out,

the circus ends,

no place for runaway fantasy.

Respite slips in honest sleep,

a fitful impermanence declawed.

Verse 34

Leavening matters in winter,

Golem knows more than one

caring mystery chilled approach,

bitters reclined in egg dipped salinate.

We dare to bless earth fruits,

mark questions, finally.

You can twist that burly, surly tongue all you like,

but we won't miss the deal,

clarifying bewilderment.

Verse 35

Golem rearranges xylem, phloem,

recites liquidambar and jacaranda,

plosive hints with fricative freckles

are pronounced defiantly from a top deck.

Drama is hoodwinked by deciduous equanimity.

You can correct me, if it makes you feel better,

but inner songs won't be denied.

Golem and I can be big and small and not at all.

Put that in your bland pipe.

Smoke away, steely apparitions.

Verse 36

Balancing me, first, on your shoulders, Golem,

we race through the thicket,

four trips' worth of holy sacs strapped across us,

long handled soft nets in all hands.

Sweeping in wide turns,

we scoop up the smallest animals,

bring them to the breathing fields, past hills,

offset altogether from captors,

plenty of grazing.

The third go round, tendons lengthen,

my feet, firm on your scapulae, hold me up.

Strength is no surprise,

we can't hurt each other,

nothing is wrong,

no bad will come,

it's alright,

here we go.

As the beloveds say,

there, there.

Verse 37

The littlest animals all gone, lanky predators howl.

Golem, we can't do it all, responsibility inflated.

Something in the cycles swoops in,

brings bony beasts their rightful meals,

no one is wracked with guilt.

Those aren't lettuce teeth and noses in ecclesiastic everydays.

We check in, breathe, depart satisfied.

Verse 38

Boiling water barefoot,

listening for the cat to meander downstairs

and stand with me,

I am unsure, Golem,

how the locked kitchen door opens honeysuckle,

pushes nobody to share the polynoses,

hinges laughing as I trip on roller skate straps.

You realize I entertain no imaginary friends,

try to right things in chalk

on another uneven sidewalk.

Arrivals continue.

Thing One and Thing Two were damn cruel.

You hear me tell of my sympathy with the trapped goldfish.

The cat is in the kitchen.

No hat, we sigh, exhaling.

Verse 39

We are having a moment.

It could be a chilly Shabbat.

Then, I ask,

> *What do you think about spiritual utilitarianism, Golem?*
>
> *The greatest good for the greatest number, in the afterlife,*
>
> *where or when every soul is created equal,*
>
> *has a fair pacifist shot.*

I explain, wait, look eagerly at you.

You are swinging your legs, eating a bag of chips,

one eyebrow raised, hands sticky with curiosity.

> *A fair shot at what?*

You ask, amused, kind.

> *Isn't death what humans call the great equalizer, anyway?*

You continue, fists full of chips,

> *And, if we're not talking about redemption, what, then?*

Considering you, your responsiveness,

I put my hands on my temples, close my eyes.

I look up, again.

The trees are bare, the radio plays top 40 hits from 1982.

I have a tape of all of this, the little scenes I've concocted.

One way to take myself less seriously, while taking life to heart,
accumulated.

Pass the crunchy.

Verse 40

We slide onto the empty narthex floor, sidestepping crystal goblets held by statues of naive knaves. Compelled to touch sculpted walls, hide and seek, Golem. How the cloistered fascination began, I'm only partly sure. Something about candles out, books closed, windows open.

Verse 41

Scintillation means, Golem,

that we have agreed to keep hush bones chiseled,

sheened with resins known.

To climb out of these skins, we swallow slowly.

Deliberate, we continue, never shallow,

beholden only to each other's resonances.

Verse 42

Golem, you remind me that people in warm climes

count their hottest evenings,

each year aim predictions

for their first three digit Fahrenheit Noon,

so it's in no way a shocker, you whisper,

or maybe all that interesting, you say gently,

leaning way down, cupping my ear with a mitten palm,

that we awaken northward,

take notice of this first two cold breaths morning,

tired skies frosted,

cloud traffic.

We near silvered grasses and oak limbs,

know a few of the voles crawling to dormancy,

nod to the spiders,

among us all a good company,

across the living, the come and gone, the not yet.

Mindful morning lullabies, from you, branching.

Verse 43

You were nearby, Golem, when I was afraid of
backwards carousels, mirror peeled faces,
suddenly slick streets, inventive bullies,
spinning animated eyes, gloomy tall night shapes,
speed on certain stairwells, my own footing.

Frogged beside me, noses pressing wonder glass,
we watched the mantis
leaping at the terrarium string meat,
you met every door frame katydid
and their grasshopper car roof cousins.
It was your idea to empty teeming ladybug bags,
freed to the garden.

I wasn't raised by three bears or pigs, an owl and a cat, or even a goose,
but they all helped.

When the tulgey wood calls my name, now, I call yours.

Verse 44

You and I talk, Golem, about bodies forgotten,
disconnects heralded by spatial confusion,
temperate clarity exchanged for undefined cognition
that solely insides find discernible,
willed cells related to others, with choices
(if that's what they're called) made solitary.
We lose track, on purpose, of how many times
we ask about what defines aliveness, interested in
sensate holism rather than fake thinking intimacy.
Not bearing witness idly, when demands arise
to know how things unfolded, why this or that was allowed,
we answer:

That is how things want to be.

Verse 45

Some tales I tell you, Golem,

are remembered hungry,

were learned without reading.

Recitation can be integrative

or promote separation,

depending upon context.

I thank you for being

with listening.

Verse 46

Wrapped around a mug, sipping green tea,

you say, Golem,

that although no, the volatile sous chef,

is sometimes a kind of proud yes,

a paradigm change maker,

and yes has been thieved sometimes

to seem complicit when it was undermined, even coerced,

because it had indeed meant no,

it's not true always that nothing makes sense.

Nothing has value, I agree,

especially in places like nowhere emptied.

We know where not to go as much as where to go,

playing filet, and other reclaimed games.

I didn't murder anyone, including you.

It was just a dream.

Death, sunk low in her chariot,

steers clear of the tower, patient, with us.

No need to hurry.

Pour some more.

Verse 47

We could open a late night diner, you suggest, Golem.

Yeah, it would be a ton of work, you add, smiling.

We could serve oddball food, healthy shakes.

At reasonable prices, have some fun.

You're trying to cheer me up on this sleepy trap morning.

We welcome the early underwater train.

Rust, glow, shimmy creaking, it will not leave without us.

When awakening worries about
what didn't, what isn't, what might,
stale cake layers outward options,
while better choices find themselves
under a close by burning bush.
Easy, warm hues invite late falls.

We spill a few crayons, sketch a menu.

Verse 48

Golem, your spaciousness calls forth lapis moths,

who land on our upturned wrists.

Delight wading in air, washing antennae.

Primeval begins every day, though not always like this,

fringed elements sinking in fern soils,

moss rugs spread for the emergent reunion.

Sprig confetti startles none of the serpent celebrants.

Monkeys watching from above enjoy their subtle fruits,

maxillary as we.

Verse 49

Once in awhile, Golem, we defog, disprefer, undo. Summoning songs, we heed indigos dispersed above and one solid squirrel below. Gray toes stopped on gray shingles, she arrives exactly, savors a small acorn I can see from my own perch. In this fitless pause, clear despair cannot steal from me, I learn to grip sustenance balanced in the apex dawn.

Verse 50

It's raining,

not simply when we permit it,

reliant on attitude

and circumstance,

while dismay is a reply anticipated,

some pine for a downpour,

cannot buoy, puff in its missing strokes.

Pacing with undimmed lenses

beside a violet chorus,

tempest Golem refracts.

Verse 51

Golem reveals electrical adjacencies,

signed dimensional mixtures,

nascent techniques

honing sensory variance.

Foolhardy desire peels partitions,

atomizes vanished lines,

reappears as winter's scars,

taut bringing torn in the seeking.

Verse 52

A young wizard confers with Golem,

hastens advice for how to address mean friends,

magic notwithstanding.

Golem considers her querent,

lips lit with thin lengths of straw.

Wisdom does not the absence of cruelty guarantee, she says,

imaging axioms, intentions whole.

But the wizard grows impatient with our fable,

runs through rocks,

no lies left or right.

Golem hums, looks around to find me,

we knot a hammock canopy promise.

Verse 53

Galloping ahead of me

in deep rows of corn,

Golem flares periwinkle,

softens peripheral danger.

We stop for savory talk

over almonds, raisins, and rice.

Putting aside cumin and saffron clockworks,

we sled later,

snowless.

Verse 54

Sized up time

packed in smooth inks

is drawn to sail.

Golem hopscotches poker, checkers, backgammon.

Glossy cards bridge shuffling to juggling.

Ambivalence about aquaria aside,

we know no nautilus visit happens,

except by passing street signs.

Maybe that chemistry building really was a flash cube,

near the oak held up honestly with my bare hands.

Don't spill any beans over candied lands from this height,

Golem cautions,

Someone could get hurt without training

in the proper use of ladders and chutes.

The mystery of how that seesaw flew against the tide

with its swinging comrades

will not be solved today.

Affairs transmogrified,

here peers a salty lighthouse business.

Verse 55

Embankment follows the blizzard voyage,

tidy in treachery,

won't last, even imprinted.

There is no fair share,

you don't get what you pay for,

buck up,

we're all steep on curves.

Golem tells it like it is.

Frolic, she insists,

you think you're short on peace.

Make yourself bigger one more time,

air out the room,

say each of your mirror names.

Slowed guard rails shuck linear effort.

The wreckage on its chain links lifts,

a stunning drink.

Verse 56

Antimacassars are somewhere, likely in their original bags,

neat needles singing to horse reigns wound round boxes looming.

My friend's crocheted tallis is there, too.

And, not just bone knit threads, gnawed embroidered bits,

but speakers I won't use,

near glass collected and PEZ dispensed.

You're right, Golem,

while associations mostly neither better nor worsen,

a few allay.

Verse 57

When this part of our passage ends, Golem, I may need you to gesture
to plexus, remind me we're not fabricated, all adventures surpassed
placating. Within sought and survived manifests, frayed or seamless,
I don't care if anyone notices. But, they won't. You'll know how to
signal, maybe burst yellow, a whistle optional.

Verse 58

Golem, I know you recall the last time Jupiter rang the bell,

asked about moving light.

We replied,

four lithe Oz horses,

two toady tympana,

Walt's body electric,

and an expectant Pan walking the plank, backwards.

That day, we waved goodbye to the chess board and the Red Queen, having just discovered Horton was too busy to hatch eggs, was no longer looking after Whos who were looking after themselves.

You paused to stop Hook.

Calming skittish Borrowers, who would not play croquet with Alice's feline anywhere near their grandfather clock filled with postage stamp art and spooled chairs,

you abated fear to move light.

Verse 59

Golem, learning has to be the day after Snap and Crackle
deflate pithy worry, no need for Pop. Recipes as yet unknown, cherries,
leeks, potatoes appear, grit rinsed. Random and planned thanks about
us, we set a new finish, my teacup synapses serene.

Verse 60

Golem says that poison in the long haul with repose is not bound by a
coupon apology, redeemed to win vesseled trouble, tomorrow.
This contraption like a shorter drawn life lot exceeds and loses in
tandem, its secular grace hope's intercessor.
If and when we do the puzzle, again, we may get identical outcomes with
different results, completion a goal assailed.
Tie the bows, hem your brushed brown trousers.
Lean in, I'm here.

Verse 61

Golem is a dandelion

blown away over sanctified ducks in a row.

Forget embattled glory, loss, or luck,

lying there, new idioms.

For you,

twelve zones multiply five elementals,

add one grass blade,

turn good six plus aught into seventh heaven.

2. Golem, Twilight

Golem, Twilight 1

The face picks itself up off the floor, shot full of hope and fur.

We were afraid momentarily of unedited twilight's chin resting
its green eyes on us.

I don't start again, I don't continue, there's nothing new in this
bitten negative.

What does trying mean for you, my friend, guileless, guilt gone, childless?

Golem, I thought I was addressing you and then remembered
you were talking to me.

I don't always know what we are, so I ask you,

where is everywhere?

Golem, Twilight 2

We meet pulled over near an empty bench as degrees drop.
I'm not sure if I can be seated.
One word, defeated, lunges without need to darken coffee
skies by the egalitarian riverbed.
Golem, you know the blurry roads, slanted pylons,
low birds flying that way.
We enjoy these bent noticings.
It's grey,
dim bright,
as above so below.

Golem, Twilight 3

Golem, you say that even if everything
smoothed to the same color,
and that color was red, we would still sense
the flush cardinal air, the flagging ship, the barnyard.
Uneven sheets would round the bend, quicken cold,
the stairs might get to us, later and later,
vented in noisy heat.
In this flaxen orbit, no amount of fresh chicken
would satisfy the little waiting carnivores,
washing their Valentine faces, expectantly.
Here comes the wrestling spectacle.
Winged chaos throws down caution, hurls control,
lies spiked and spiced, all done.
At my head and feet, on either side of me,
pens helped as much as kid angels could.
Right, you say, what did I expect?
Your story makes me laugh, riding a stationary cycle.

Golem, Twilight 4

Snow falling lightly teaches silence.
Golem and I watch, lose count.
Knots unravel at the old cordoned theater,
its backdrop a pumpkin compost.
Disappear, the flakes insist,
you're not really here.
No mystics own alone the soil under unidentical trees turning white.
Circle work, ephemeral, underlines its pleasures, melts.

Golem, Twilight 5

Rumor has it that the first to speak was a spoon, spaghetti, dada, or no. Golem thinks I can vote for no. No, slicker than spaghetti, stranger than dada, more persuasive than a spoon. No bows, tips a hat, says so what to Aleph, who splits into three in her nascent sea. Scraps paddle a boat, pass out, come to, full grown.

Golem, Twilight 6

If a chamber ensemble begins by way of a nautilus, instead of in a
congress, what cool might the mantle bring? You can't never mind
politics, Golem, you wanted to meet Neruda's questions, woodwinds
brittle, uncorked. The shiniest slime trails the corrugated crag on
musseled Maine. Siphons spit to pennies that don't belong and are not
good luck for anyone shelled. Many look to evergreen, and sometimes
I do, too, but here I squint down, ask the barely there snails what it's like
to be human. Opening each operculum, they eddy spineless jokes.
Golem grins, thinking of squid, audacious. Years of our moods,
in malacology.

Golem, Twilight 7

Golem, before breakfast, language rails on.
Retroflex implosives echo inner wars.
Pleasure articulates occlusion.
Without outlets, we stop to create them.
Palates summon, resolute, unpronounced.
Airstreams can travel across country,
painterly and piecemeal,
but I choose breathing, first.
Alfa, Bravo, and Charlie,
we'll meet you at the Delta.

Golem, Twilight 8

You are yourself, entirely, but I'm not even sure who that is.
I don't want or have to figure this out. Thank goodness.
Two of the best parts of the world we inhabit, Golem,
are the surprises and unknowing.
When I think of pinball, chewing gum, resonant tones
in copper bells, you resemble focus.
What does not reckon or beckon may still remind.
Even the saddest instant shifts.
Well deep and ridges earned, proof is in the pudding.

Golem, Twilight 9

Helpless freedom cracks open possibility, destroyed teachings
photosynthesized. Break the let go welcomes shelled. Golem and I
cross the bridge. Where are the seagulls going? We all want to know.
Spirals are misunderstood by delimited perception. You want to go
check that vertical buckling mylar again. If it's still there. Better to
revisit the fun house than the haunted mansion or even the freak show.
There's that railing above the no sitting here sign. We laugh sweetly at
the 110 camera with its marigold button in a pristine case strapped
opposite a French fry holster belting highwaters over flat feet that never
got to plummet from the parachute, a fossil before you were born.
Centripetal force, cross cut roast beef sandwiches, and dread may be
gone, but the boardwalk meets the wind forever. Dead hits first, glows
second. Home run.

Golem, Twilight 10

Longest moonlight,
no coffee,
overthrown quilted baroque,
still life with irises and nightshade.
Golem paces beside me; I move less and less.

Golem, Twilight 11

If you could save this world, Golem, how would you proceed?
I can, you tell me. *I can, and I will.* You rise up gathered, so serious, your
fists way above your head. Clearly, you've been considering this mission
for some time, maybe even waiting for me to ask. You say, *I have to begin*
by shutting all the sensory doors, I must open them anew, spit fire fountains, after
breathing for years underground in the last sharp cave I will have dug for myself,
listening to the plants animals rocks seas hills, their choices delivered at once, as they
desire nonwords, and, having prioritized them, including bacteria and protozoa
soothed, turn then to the people and their virus cousins who remain clinging cliffside
after the melted ice caps have dissolved fully. Promises kept in devoted shapeshifts,
plates tectonic no more, there will be boundless, noiseless hastening, volcanism through
brandished ores will anew create landforms and foods equitably under sun number
three. Then, you laugh so loud, ask how much longer we have to play this
silly game before getting Chinese food on Christmas. No heresy protest,
merely an outsider party. *So, c'mon*, you stare at me, *let's unfurl the scarves*
without messiahs and enjoy a few hot noodles.

Golem, Twilight 12

Golem skips open gently the lids of a series
of unsequenced bottles.
Their necks breathe out,
return untightened to a premise of surrender.
No promises exist, no hope,
just the fact of messy love accepted.

You can't grasp openness.

Golem, Twilight 13

There are no grief stages, Golem reminds me, no performances, no order. Rhyme and reason are not feminized, she says, do not need to be and are not rescued on the flip side of any tollbooth, phantom or otherwise. If you upset the tame cat, you'll get bitten, because there is no such thing as a tame cat. You either keep facing squarely, or you can cut out life, and, even if you go at it, the eventual terminus hits, and it sure as hell isn't in Coney Island. At that final stop, after a long bus ride, only the waiting car gets to the edge of the places to visit, at last. Nowhere to sit, you hang on to the end of the year, trying not to bother or to be bothered, then travel unpaved, like it or not. For now, buckle up, boy scout, and roll, knowing, wherever you are and however you get there, when you picture one mile lit up, it will be measured in city blocks from the Village to Chelsea. Before the hipster takeover, you went to grit world, romanceless. Fear and honesty aren't always friends. Unless you are a cat bite.

Golem, Twilight 14

The cat slinks around the wild hearth and tools, black iron clangs and a
puffed out tail greeting. He's been holding court in the kitchen, too, on
stove alert for weeks. After I wrote of the voles approaching dormancy,
one showed up. Golem winks, calls me a conjurer. Two rescued, one
found posthumous, over the years since making this home. Tiny clever
four will perhaps teach me when best to climb the walls.

Golem, Twilight 15

Golem curls up beside the sleeping ouroboros.

Waves freeze mid-air.

Fire fronts its exchanged elementals.

Vines lift around rising sea smoke.

Knowing I need a dragon smile.

Golem, Twilight 16

The scene nests the day.

Cloudless, Golem sinks into wet sand, eels underfoot, rock slip.

Birds grasp their own tails above a thickening undertow.

Fire horses resigned know strange bliss in gaits unstable.

Sing. You can do it.

Faces lying over the ocean return the narrow bridge to brethren.

Night is unbroken taffy.

Start spreading the news, she's not leaving today.

Golem, Twilight 17

Golem considers when done happens.

Medium rare steak, marrow suck, vole snack, shit silver,
cat shred chicken, ink eye,

stir the frozen pea pot,

you fluent Sneetch.

Golem, Twilight 18

Golem enjoys medical terminology, never pretends prefixes could have prevented a damned thing. Bunny buntings break their boughs, ditch for dancing, move the mega moons. Sickness familiar doesn't make it known. A stranger tissued kindness leads to bedded hallways admitting no one. Haze captions maroon.

Golem, Twilight 19

Met with street falafel pacing, jump lights raise spirits
to a favored bridge music.

Vole rests on Golem palms, stories segmented,

possibly takes someone's place as a karmic favor.

Shelled sunflowers in the corner drawer cleaned,
doors swell open.

You have to pull really hard, but I can still get here from there.

Good to talk back to grizzle and pith returned.

Hold tight the bar to cross under Styx balloons.

Golem, Twilight 20

Golem, please craft us a paw pad day.

Caramelize shallot and garlic,

add spinach with tomatoes sliced,

lay down eggs whipped,

melt cheese, fold.

Toast crumpets, heat mocha.

Even though none can be made whole.

Golem, Twilight 21

Fissures in found wood match vertical floor to ceiling cracks gaze to foundation seep speak with Golem who for me translates it is a lot and you can park orange buoys beside swans gliding across the street.

Golem, Twilight 22

Joist creek, wide angle rasp.

Coins pocket turn, jute tightens, engine clicks.

Golem knows Lucy's been in the sky
for more than half a century,

scooping licorice from a dirigible.

We marble fish, crucible shut, miss the shoulder boat.

Golem, Twilight 23

Godwink trifecta, pantheon lure.

Underworld tricks fast and lean,

diagrams meaty answering to a higher authority.

Cursing the ephemeris, a waste of time.

Litany gateway cannot stop acacia gum mythography.

Golem haunches, spits.

Red light,   one Mississippi,

      ready or not,

              two Mississippi,

green light,

          all dressed in black,

      here we come.

Golem, Twilight 24

Grain heavy moon sack drops one eyed to teat knees.

Golem dips lit planes, sky slivers.

Paper crumbles through window lines, ego shards decanter.

Blare the horns, wistful armor.

Reception in, static out.

Among splintered porcelain, bulls lick their feet,

then drive home.

Golem, Twilight 25

Onion skins off the counter,

Golem slats wood, polishes moss.

We sweep beaches, count pylons.

Agates whorl, picture jasper.

Knit one, pearl two.

Sidereal cerulean notes telescopic feathers stirring air.

Sediment agar, tectonic transduction, isomer theatrics.

Pinwheels ricochet their whiskered ceremonies.

Beneath the brass ring, sleep rides.

Golem, Twilight 26

Wisps harden, cap the double dipped cone, incomplete.

No, we cannot know why.

To avoid being pulled through desiccant, become flurries.

Basement hell may meet attic heaven, but stairs remain restrictive.

Access the floor, knees and elbows receding, odd equity.

Tuck your prehensile reminders under wet feet before resistance slips.

Kick back, enjoy ancient staging.

Golem advice on a Mars morning.

Golem, Twilight 27

What became of the Bay City Rollers? Let's thank them for introducing weird fifth graders to tartan salves. Golem was in the wings when heartthrob detective had to mean male. We not boys got teased as Encyclopedia Browns, before nerds were cool, used hole punched catalogs full of famously punished fags like us. Bewitched was all sorts of validation, years ahead of outlier card reading. Pixie dust arrived in sweet straws. Gum served by zebras, shaped like burger toppings, fell out of crocodile jaws, wrapped in tiny record sleeves protected by the most valuable players.

Golem, Twilight 28

Dawn propellers criss crossed, beads crimson.

Golem builds diaramas, castaway dolls sew lineage.

Snark arrives, hunting unnecessary.

Hindsight is rhubarb, associations strawberry preserved stick.

Golem, Twilight 29

Twister down the flue,
up the century maple,
acrobat a darker grey than the others,
soot prints across the stove,
cabinet curious.

Golem daffodil sings.

Golem, Twilight 30

Absent fifty pages, rake coals lickety split.

Eulogy caboose leaps off the rails.

Ashes mix shale to shoal,

Golem pulleys the well bucket decade.

Don't ever stop looking hazel,

my Mercury right here.

Golem, Twilight 31

Reading Le Guin (may she rest as she wishes),
Golem recalls with me the untamed cat nights,
unable to be summoned.
We have one.
I profess my love to the cat, who stares then nips.
I tell him we use different languages,
knowing he understands everything I'm not saying,
and possibly some of what I just did.
I'll never be fluent, but we could discuss
how snails fly through water,
chasing microbes on kelp backs,
cat tails keeping watch in the algae.
When yogurt, symphonic not sedentary,
gets lapped up, dancing.
That arms and arms and arms
of pelagic invertebrates are peaceful in salty rims.
Which otters know what penguins.
What flamingos meet where.
Eating Centella asiatica,
when elephants memorize ant collaboration.
People, the infamy infantry,
are not only not better than nonhumans,
we bite.
At least that's what I think the cat said.

Golem, Twilight 32

Traffic is defined by unrealistic expectations,
Golem says, salt fingers.
Smooth illusory motion bullshit.

Our braided pretzel dialogue is vulgar.
Pause another memoir featuring addiction
with a puffin sticker.
Ruskin was right about the penguins
and nothing being too serious
when considering them.

Puffins are penguins lit up legal speed,
I parry, smoking a pretzel.

She wasn't raised by inconsolable punchcutters.
And didn't grow up. Advantages of being
incarnate undead. Once she met Athena
and they discussed that crap the men made up
about the girl not having a mother,
born full from her father's mind.
If you bring that up, again, you'll get an earful.

Golem is night blooming cereus,
the poppies,
Devil's claws dried,
a car seat in between trees asleep.
Is the cool wedding band above anklet socks
protection sinking to the living room.
Is the snow smoke road white knuckle drive back.
Is as misunderstood as viper seer sweetness.

Golem, Twilight 33

The following morning, looking glass quiet, bold diffusion, Golem saw
her passing under the seeds from sewn to ashen Neptune, showed me
how the ordinary mystical news carries, each to each, on ice shelved leaf
pod winds, the whole spread sea, communitas elf touch tipping gravity.

Golem, Twilight 34

Your turbulent mother calls you home as we break light to blue.
There is nothing to empty if it's all inside, I tell Golem.
The Green Man welcomes Lilith,
newts glide the Hudson,
owls raise the subway.
Sure, that's what Tiggers like.
Even a cookie reminds me of you.

Golem, Twilight 35

Waking up where I'll likely never sleep, again,
Capote's profile frames the library dismantled,
paper plates disposed, pens dried up,
shirts arranged for strangers.

Your absence ruins the ocean, for now.

We stackers can't find that one metal teapot.

Golem in the glass chimes takes down the sun.

Golem, Twilight 36

Decoupaged hat, you left, too.

We move the little rolltop desk for two fallen angels,
one of whom is a poet.

You sent us Rilke, anyway.

There was no surface unadorned,
your daughter who knows she doesn't know
what it isn't, said, flying.

Golem, please pack my bags full of the last time,
I'm stuck on my bug back, I need help.

Golem, Twilight 37

A dragonfly around my neck saw you go over the new moon.
You can see these days in the dark,
speak in mind sweeps,
whistle through us.
Golem, in compass clothing, points me
to your dropped bougainvillea bract.
Disintegrated at the baggage station,
magenta remains in my pocket.

Golem, Twilight 38

Absence sits at fathomless breakfast.

A rabbit wakes up Golem, who arranges your jewelry.

I am written on my hands.

The snow goose joins a chamsa.

Golem, Twilight 39

Lachrymose cranes soak through a clean poem,
split the Jamestown and Buffalo sun peach strip.

Golem deflects the hundredth solar plexus punch.

Salamanders charge, slow, lean, and low, volley neutral to amber,
approach crickets camouflaged.

Oleander's pretty poisons fanned away when we rinsed chard using a
hamper colander after you explained that thrown jade can root
anywhere.

We talked quietly to ants and snails, poured cement stepped confidence.

Glass edges, clamps, rolls of black tape, vats of glue, you know what was
in there, replete the refashioned leavetaking, wood and paper too open
to be secular Jericho.

Even so, I'm glad you met her at the last culvert
before the decades of cohesive disassemblage.

3. Golem Daffodils

Golem Daffodils 1

Back in thin time, Golem dreamed secular blessings.
Bass lines underscored a fool, the high priestess consort.
Wicked sickle teeth, etch-pointed, betrayed no cautions.
Impoverished fluidity was never an issue
for pirate pentacle queens.
Dust cacophony revolutions dried in reverse.
Scooping up lichen, I swallowed learnings, readied for later.
Saving delight -- or daylight -- a lie,
desire unattached the far better fae bet.
Push me, pull, you may have known your dendrites,
but left, nonetheless,
great pink sea snail faces indelible.

Golem Daffodils 2

A whole fish swivel clef loosens molly bolts.
Music turns on itself.
Anchors refuse walls, chisel inward,
banished before invocation.
Petal tipped east, Golem fog averts, empties pipelines.
Clean tricks, soil bent, parts teeming with timing.
Ice caps unmelt, bears tilt Polaris.
Spill away, run off,
neutrino effervescent bisons spin integers to bosons become.
Halfway frenetic fermions play.

Golem Daffodils 3

Air anvils apparate photographs,
agar raiment waves dissolve.
Golem microbe slides,
one stink bug wall sleet surfs.
Big cats summit Barbary sheep, circadian.
Limp or crisp, nobody eats
this cumulus night.

Golem Daffodils 4

Hammer feet sidle tawny seams,
curled behind a mist teal desk,
hasp washed.
Eager, eared,
wheel scavenger training.
Camera obscura mash reveals
pasty compost,
gnash ready.
Golem calls, incisive.

Golem Daffodils 5

Tail tip swish impersonates thickness,
Golem hears me advised that no one is seeking to intrude on life.
The point of it all is not to ask about the point,
just to be in the middle of right now, without being right, now,
as now is right. Diastema windy is not a real whistle, so what,
wings open, hatch struts. Quarter rests, half rests, sustained,
take notes, no prisoners.

Golem Daffodils 6

Reading Neruda, we portmanteau, too much tea before bed.

Golem cloaks strings pulleyed from the wellspring porter.

The civil quest minds the gap.

How many volts does it take
to glisten the center of a ghastly room?

> *Down down baby*
> *Down by the roller coaster.*

Do you know exactly how to eat your words?

> *Sweet sweet baby*
> *I'll never let you go.*

If Miss Lucy had a gremlin she named yesterday,
would troubles still seem far away?

> *Shimmy shimmy cocoa pop*
> *Shimmy shimmy pow.*

About Diane R. Wiener

Diane R. Wiener's forays into poetics have been read by her, publicly, as well as used by friends as adapted dramatic monologues. Although Diane has written poetry since she was seven, prior to her first full-length collection, *The Golem Verses*, she had published relatively few of her poems: at age nine, in *Archie Comics* and *Child Life*; at 39, in a now defunct online interdisciplinary journal of science and literature; and, shortly before her 51st birthday, in the Spring 2017 issue of *Nine Mile Art & Literary Magazine*. 15 selections from *The Golem Verses* were published in Nine Mile's Spring 2018 issue (an invited anthology); four selections from the book manuscript were also published in the June 2018 issue of *Wordgathering: A Journal of Disability Poetry and Literature*.

In addition to her love of poetry, Diane self-identifies as an educator, social worker, advocate, singer, bassist, and artist, among other roles. She has longstanding commitments to mindfulness, interfaith and secular contemplation, humanism, and exegesis. Diane has published widely on issues related to social justice, pedagogy, and empowerment. She blogged for the *Huffington Post* between May, 2016 and January, 2018.

Diane is the full-time Director of the Syracuse University Disability Cultural Center, and she teaches part-time for the Renée Crown University Honors Program, also at S.U.